WALKING
THE CHESHIRE RING
by
John N. Merrill.

Maps and photographs by John N. Merrill.

a J.N.M. Publication

1990

a J.N.M. PUBLICATION,

J.N.M. PUBLICATIONS,
WINSTER,
MATLOCK,
DERBYSHIRE.
DE4 2DQ
℗ Winster (062988) 454
Fax: Winster (062988) 416

Concieved, edited, typeset, designed, paged, marketed and distributed by John N. Merrill.

© Text and route - John N. Merrill 1990.

© Maps and photographs - John N. Merrill 1990.

First Published -   April 1990.

ISBN 0 907496 63 6

Meticulous research has been undertaken to ensure that this publication is highly accurate at the time of going to press. The publishers, however, cannot be held responsible for alterations, errors or omissions, but they would welcome notification of such for future editions.

Typeset in - Bookman - bold, italic and plain 9pt and 18pt.

Printed by -   Black Bear Press Ltd., Cambridge.

Cover Sketch by John Creber - Trent & Mersey Canal near Rode Heath. © J.N.M. PUBLICATIONS 1990.

ABOUT
JOHN N. MERRILL

John combines the characteristics and strength of a mountain climber with the stamina and athletic capabilities of a marathon runner. In this respect he is unique and has to his credit a whole string of remarkable long walks. He is without question the world's leading marathon walker.

Over the last fifteen years he has walked more than 100,000 miles and successfully completed ten walks of a least 1,000 miles or more. His six major walks in Great Britain are -

<blockquote>
Hebridean Journey....... 1,003 miles.
Northern Isles Journey......913 miles.
Irish Island Journey ....1,578 miles.
Parkland Journey.......2,043 miles.
Land's End to John o' Groats.....1,608 miles.
</blockquote>

and in 1978 he became the first person (permanent Guinness Book of Records entry) to walk the entire coastline of Britain - 6,824 miles in ten months.

In Europe he has walked across Austria - 712 miles - hiked the Tour of Mont Blanc, completed High Level Routes in the Dolomites and Italian Alps, and the GR20 route across Corsica in training! In 1982 he walked across Europe - 2,806 miles in 107 days - crossing seven countries, the Swiss and French Alps and the complete Pyrennean chain - the hardest and longest mountain walk in Europe, with more than 600,000 feet of ascent!

In America he used The Appalachian Trail - 2,200 miles - as a training walk, He has walked from Mexico to Canada via the Pacific Crest Trail in record time - 118 days for 2,700 miles. He has walked most of the Continental Divide Trail and much of New Mexico; his second home. In Canada he has walked the Rideau Trail - Kingston to Ottowa - 220 miles and The Bruce Trail - Tobermory to Niagara Falls - 460 miles.

In 1984 John set off from Virginia Beach on the Atlantic coast, and walked 4,226 miles without a rest day, across the width of America to Santa Cruz and San Francisco on the Pacific coast. His walk is unquestionably his greatest achievement, being, in modern history, the longest, hardest crossing of the U.S.A. in the shortest time - under six months (178 days). The direct distance is 2,800 miles.

Between major walks John is out training in his own area - The Peak District National Park. He has walked all of our National Trails many times - The Cleveland Way thirteen times and The Pennine Way four times in a year! He has been trekking in the Himalayas five times. He created more than a dozen challenge walks which have been used to raise more than £250,000 for charity. From his own walks he has raised over £100,000. He is author of more than one hundred walking guides; most of which he publishes himself, His book sales are in excess of 2 1/2 million, He has created many long distance walks including The Limey Way , The Peakland Way, Dark Peak Challenge walk, and Rivers' Way. He lectures extensively in Britain and America.

CONTENTS

INTRODUCTION

The Cheshire Ring is one of the greatest canal circuits in Britain, linking together the Ashton, Rochdale, Bridgewater, Trent & Mersey, Macclesfield, and Peak Forest canals together. Almost all lies within the Cheshire boundary and whilst being flat country, the scenery is varied and spectacular -from the hills to the plains and through industrial complexes. The canal provides a tranquil setting in the most urban development. The variety found on the walk is almost unique and is a remarkable cross section of modern life while following a transport route more than 200 years old.

I had long wanted to walk it not just for my canal walk series but to discover its history and view familiar places from new angles. For ease of compiling the book I walked it in stages. I did 20 - 24 miles a day and being level walking found I could do this easily and overtake the narrowboats as well! The sun shone every day and it only rained after I had completed the last section! Incredible as it may seem, apart from passing three people walking their dogs, I met no other walkers even though it was July!

It is hard to pinpoint the sections I liked best, but the Trent & Mersey has several outstanding stretches, several quite remote and totally unspoilt. The Macclesfield Canal, which you walk end to end is a gem and the Peak Forest Canal has stunning locks and an impressive aqueduct The Manchester area is a wider canal and more industrial but is nevertheless rich in history.

I look upon the walk with fond memories and hope that your walk is equally as pleasant and that the weather is fine. A plus factor for canal walking is that there are numerous inns along the way and bridges to shelter under. Have a good walk and let me know how you got on.

HAPPY WALKING,

John N. Merrill

Winster. 1990

ABOUT
THE WALKS

Whilst every care is taken detailing and describing the walks in this book, it should be borne in mind that the countryside changes by the seasons and the work of man. I have described the walks to the best of my ability, detailing what I have found on the walk in the way of stiles and signs. Obviously with the passage of time stiles become broken or replaced by a ladder stile or even a small gate. Signs too have a habit of being broken or pushed over. All the routes follow rights of way and only on rare occasions will you have to overcome obstacles in its path, such as a barbed wire fence or electric fence.

The seasons bring occasional problems whilst out walking which should also be borne in mind. In the height of summer paths become overgrown and you will have to fight your way through in a few places. In low lying areas the fields are often full of crops, and although the pathline goes straight across it may be more practical to walk round the field edge to get to the next stile or gate. In summer the ground is generally dry but in autumn and winter, especially because of our climate, the surface can be decidedly wet and slippery; sometimes even gluttonous mud!

These comments are part of countryside walking which help to make your walk more interesting or briefly frustrating. Standing in a farmyard up to your ankles in mud might not be funny at the time but upon reflection was one of the highlights of the walk!

The mileage for each walk is based on three calculations -

1. pedometer reading.
2. the route map measured on the map.
3. the time I took for the walk.

I believe the figure stated for each walk to be very accurate but we all walk differently and not always in a straight line! The time allowed for each walk is on the generous side and does not include pub stops etc. The figure is based on the fact that on average a person walks 2 1/2 miles an hours but less in hilly terrain.

ABOUT THE WALK AND HOW TO DO IT .

I have started the walk at Dukinfield on purpose, but being circular you can start it anywhere. The section along the Ashton Canal to Manchester serves as a pleasant introduction past locks and industrial buildings into the very centre of Manchester. A short piece of road walking through the city centre close to the Rochdale Canal takes you to the Bridgwater Canal, which at first is not particularly attractive but once past Old Trafford the scenery gradually improves and as the miles go by becomes stunning. At Preston Brook you leave the Bridgwater Canal and begin following the Trent & Mersey to the Macclesfield Canal at Red Bull, near Kidsgrove. Whilst the scenery on the Trent & Mersey has been very attractive and passing the fabled Anderton Lift near Northwich, the Macclesfield Canal lying beneath the western edge of the Peak District Pennine hills is breathtaking walking over many impressive canal features such as the Bosley Locks and Bollington Aqueduct. At Marple you join the Peak Forest Canal; again superlative walking past a flight locks and aqueduct and on to Dukinfield. By doing the walk from here you get the worst over first and the further along the towpath you go the more enjoyable the walk becomes.

You can do the walk in a variety of ways; as a week's walk, over several weekends or in stages when time permits. As the canals pass numerous towns and villages there are many places offering all grades of accommodation, as detailed in the amenities guide. There is no need to rush the walk, and no one is worried if you take seven or seventy days; the main thing is to enjoy it. Apart from central Manchester, which I mapped fully, you can walk the route using the Ordnance Survey 1:50,000 series and the whole walk is covered by sheets Numbers -

109 - Manchester and Surrounding area.
108 - Liverpool and Surrounding area.
117 - Chester, Wrexham and Surrounding area.
118 - Stoke on Trent and Macclesfield area.

J.N.M. Publications keeps a master record of all those who complete the walk using this guide and issues a special John Merrill Canal Walk badge and signed certificate to all those successfully completing the walk.

JAMES BRINDLEY - 1716 -1772

James Brindley, the greatest canal engineer of his time, was born at Tunstead, near Wormhill, Derbyshire. At Wormhill is a drinking trough to his memory. He was uneducated and could hardly read or write. From an early age he was fascinated by mechanical things. He saw a corn mill and sketched the parts to understand how it worked. At the age of 17 he went to work for a millwright, named Abraham Bennett, at Sutton near Macclesfield. He soon showed a natural talent for designing mechanical works using water. He earned himself a nickname - 'the schemer' - for his now apparent genius. On one occasion he worked at a mill on one of the Duke of Bridgewater's estates.

His skill soon reached the ears of the Duke, and so began one of the major partnerships in transportation. The Duke needed engineering advice, for he wanted to move coal from his mines on the Worsley estate to the port of Manchester. He had devised a canal but was stuck at making locks. Brindley suggested an aqueduct, which was thought unrealistic by the establishment. But the Duke could see it was a good sound idea, and it was built - 900 yards long and 17 feet high - carrying the canal over the River Irwell at Barton. The canal was opened in 1761 and became the wonder of the year. This immediately reduced the price of coal in Manchester from 17d(7p) a hundredweight to 3 1/2d(1 1/2p).

Whilst canals were already being built for short distances, Brindley's expertise launched the country into a fervour of activity, with the next 80 years being the canal's heyday - until the advent of railways. With the Duke he went on to construct 360 miles of canals. His next project was the Manchester - Liverpool Canal, 24 miles long. Brindley was poorly paid for his work - 3s 6d(17 1/2p) a day. The labourers were getting ls 2d(6p). He went on to link Liverpool, Hull and Bristol together by waterway - The Grand Trunk system.

Others followed, such as the Birmingham Canal in 1768, the Droitwich Canal and Chesterfield Canal. Incredibly, Brindley never wrote anything down, he kept everything in his head. He simply went to bed to think it out! He died aged 56, on September 27th 1772.

> " The rugged Brindley has little to say for himself.
> He has chained the seas together. His ships do visibly
> float over valleys, and invisibly through the hearts of
> mountains; the Mersey and the Thames, the Humber
> and the Severn, have shaken hands."

Carlyle.

If you are ever in Leek, Staffordshire, I can highly recommend a visit to Brindley's water mill there. There are many fascinating items and considerable information on James Brindley and the canal era.

Brindley's Mill, Leek.

THE ASHTON CANAL

6 1/4 miles long with 18 locks.

Authorised in 1792 and opened in 1799. Principally to serve the mills in the Ashton area, it was a rival to the Rochdale Canal. The Huddersfield Narrow Canal was built later. With the construction of the Macclesfield Canal in 1831 there was a through route from Manchester to the Potteries. This was one reason the canal survived longer than most. In 1846 it was sold to the Great Central Railway. Traffic slowly declined and by 1962 it was unnavigable but in 1974 it was reopened to form an integral part of the Cheshire Ring.

Dukinfield - Peak Forest Canal aqueduct on right.

Ashton Packet Boat Co., - Guide Bridge.

Clayton Locks - Manchester in distance.

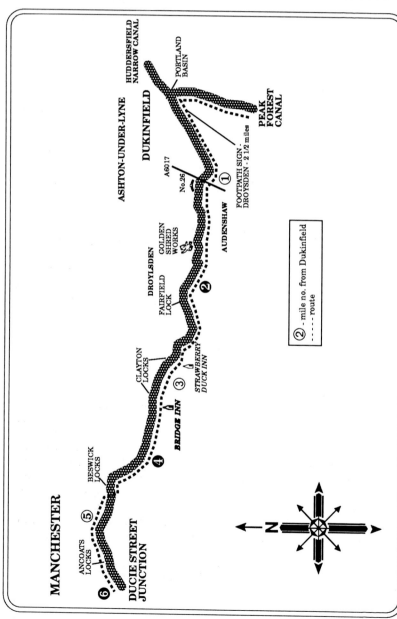

THE ASHTON CANAL
DUKINFIELD TO DUCIE STREET JUNCTION - 6 miles

HUDDERSFIELD NARROW CANAL

PORTLAND BASIN

PEAK FOREST CANAL

ASHTON-UNDER-LYNE

DUKINFIELD

A6017

No.26

①

FOOTPATH SIGN - DROYSDEN - 2 1/2 miles

AUDENSHAW

DROYLSDEN

GOLDEN SHRED WORKS

FAIRFIELD LOCK

②

CLAYTON LOCKS

STRAWBERRY DUCK INN

③

BRIDGE INN

④

BESWICK LOCKS

MANCHESTER

⑤

ANCOATS LOCKS

DUCIE STREET JUNCTION

⑥

② - mile no. from Dukinfield
- - - - route

N

12

DUKINFIELD TO DUCIE STREET JUNCTION (PICCADILLY) - 6 MILES - allow 2 1/4 hours.

CANAL - Ashton canal.

 - O.S. l:50,000 Landranger Series Sheet No 109 - Manchester &
surrounding area.
-O.S. 1:25,000 Pathfinder Series Sheet No SJ 89/99 Manchester &
Ashton-Under-Lyne.

ABOUT THE SECTION - Starting from the junction at the Portland
Basin in Dukinfield of the Ashton, Peak Forest and Huddersfield
Narrow Canals. You follow the Ashton Canal from almost rural
surroundings into the very heart of Manchester. By starting here you
get the least enjoyable section over first. The route is interesting
through industrial area and suburbia, passing 27 bridges (some
quite low) and numerous locks, including the flight of Clayton locks.
The start is a little awkward to get to. From the roundabout in
Ashton-Under-Lyne of the A635, A5017 and A662 roads, the Ashton
canal is 1/4 mile south east down a minor road to bridge No 28 just
west of the Portland Basin. Here a path sign states - Droysden 2
1/2 miles - along the canal.

WALKING INSTRUCTIONS - Gain the canal towpath and keep
the canal on your right as you walk westwards away from the Portland Basin. In 1 1/2 mile you pass under Bridge No 21 which is quite
low. Soon afterwards you pass on your right the tall chimney of the
Golden Shred works. 1/2 mile later reach the Fairfield Locks. There
are 18 locks on the canal which are collectively known as the Ashton
Flight. They comprise the Ancoats, Beswick, Clayton and Fairfield
locks. Clayton has the most with eight. Any narrowboat traversing
this section needs about seven hours to work its way through the
locks - it's quicker on foot! Keep on the canal to Ducie Street Junction
with the Rochdale Canal at Paradise Mill, close to Piccadilly Station.
The Clayton Locks are spectacular with views to central Manchester.
There are two inns here - the Bridge Inn and Strawberry Duck Inn.
On gaining the Beswick Locks the remaining bridges are quite low.

THE ROCHDALE CANAL

35 miles of main line and branches from Manchester to Sowerby Bridge.

In May 1791 £60,000 had been subscribed in an hour for a canal from Manchester to Rochdale. The route of the canal from Manchester was past Oldham to the River Roch and a branch to Rochdale. A later branch was added to Heywood. From the River Roch the canal continued into Yorkshire to Sowerby Bridge where it joined the Calder and Hebble Navigation.

The canal was authorised in 1704, survey by John Rennie and built by William Jessop. Ten years later in 1804 it was opened to traffic; the first through route across the Pennines, linking Lancashire and Yorkshire. Competition was fierce from other canals and later the railways. In 1833 a dividend of less than 5% was paid. The opening of the Leeds & Manchester Railway in March 1841 saw the start of a great battle for trade with charges being reduced. In 1888 - 686,000 tons was carried but most of this was not through traffic. Steam barges were being used in the 1900's but by 1921 the Canal Company's boats ceased to trade.

Boats using the canal were a maximum of 72 feet long with a capacity of 70 tons. It took 7 hours from Manchester to Rochdale, ascending 41 locks. In the early days "fly boats" were used offering a speedy service, carrying 20 tons. A night service was operated between Manchester and Todmorden with a capacity of 12 tons.

When the canals came to be nationalised in 1948 it was excluded like several others including the Derby Canal. In 1952 it was abandoned. The two mile part through central Manchester from Castlefields - the end of the Bridgewater Canal - and Ducie Street Junction - the junction with the Ashton Canal -has been maintained enabling the Cheshire Ring to be navigable.

Rochdale Canal - central Manchester.

Castlefields Junction, Manchester.

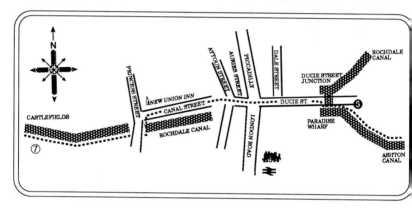

Cheshire Ring sign nr. Grocer's warehouse.

Rochdale Canal nr. Castlefields.

DUCIE STREET JUNCTION TO CASTLEFIELDS - 1 MILE
- allow 20 minutes.

CANAL - ROCHDALE

 - 0.5. 1:50,000 Landranger Series sheet No 109 - Manchester & surrounding area.

- O.S. 1:25,000 Pathfinder Series Sheet No SJ 89/99 Manchester & Ashton-Under-Lyne.

ABOUT THE SECTION - Through the very heart of Manchester, despite the tall buildings and numerous roads, the canal is a tranquil haven and a wonderful way to pass through a city.

WALKING INSTRUCTIONS - At Paradise Wharf - Ducie Street Junction - where the Ashton and Rochdale canals meet, turn right to the road Ducie Street and turn left along it. It is not possible to follow the canal at this point. Walk along Ducie Street to the Piccadilly/London Road. Go straight across and along Auries street to Aytoun Street. Cross this and a small car park to reach Canal Street. Here on your left is the Rochdale Canal. There is no towpath but walk down the length of Canal Street to its end with the New Union Inn on your right. Turn left over the canal bridge and descend to the towpath. Keep on this cobbled towpath with the canal on your right all the way to Castlefields 3/4 mile away, en route passing several locks.

THE GROCERS WAREHOUSE - Built about 1775 at the end of the Bridgewater Canal and ls one of the oldest warehouses ln Manchester. The warehouse was built by Hugh Henshall, brother in law and assistant to James Brindley. In 1811 it was sold to the Manchester's Grocers company. Boats came off the canal into the centre of the building and goods were hoisted to any of the five floors. An ingenious system of water tunnels and underground waterwheels hoisted the goods.

THE BRIDGEWATER CANAL

23 1/2 miles long with one lock - Hulme Lock, Manchester.
Authorised March 23rd. 1759

The third Duke of Bridgewater, Francis Egerton, is regarded as the first person to build a modern canal. His drive and energy saw the birth of canal system in Britain. He had coal mines at Worsley near Manchester and it was expensive to have coal carried by packhorse to Manchester. His agent, John Gilbert, urged him to build a canal. An application was made to Parliament and on March 23rd 1759 it was given the Royal Assent. This was the first act for an artificial waterway that was completely independent of any river. The major proviso for granting permission was that coal would be sold in Manchester at 4d (1 1/2p) or less per cwt. This was a greatly reduced price.

James Brindley was the engineer and the first section was opened in 1761. This included the first stone built aqueduct at Barton over the River Irwell - 200 yards long and 39 feet above the river. At the time it was one of the wonders of the world to see boats travelling above the river. Water for the canal came from the colliery.

James Brindley also designed the first canal containers for transporting coal on the canal. They were made of wood and measured 6 foot x 4 1/2 feet x 4 feet deep and held 35 cwt. Ten of these containers were carried on a narrowboat about 68 feet long.

In 1762 the Duke was given permission to extend the canal from Castlefields to the Trent & Mersey Canal at Preston Brook. The canal carried commercial traffic until 1974.

Mural, Bridgewater Canal, Trafford Park.

Bridgewater Canal - Leigh Junction.

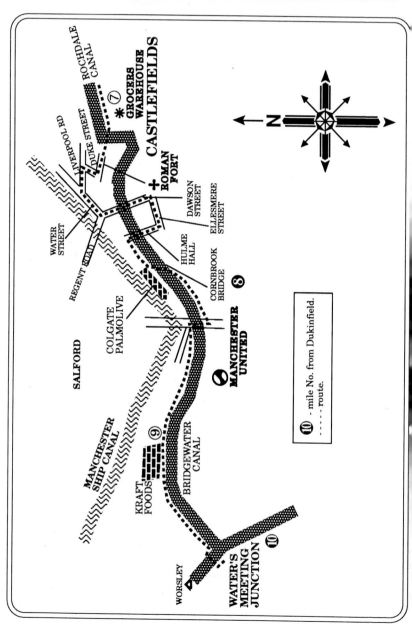

20

CANAL - BRIDGEWATER

- O.S. l:50,000 Landranger Series Sheet No 109 - Manchester & surrounding area.
- O.S 1:25,000 Pathfinder Series Sheet No SJ 89/99 Manchester & Ashton-Under-Lyne.

ABOUT THE SECTION - Leaving Manchester city centre behind you follow the Rochdale Canal past the world famous Old Trafford (Manchester united) football ground to Water's Meeting; the junction with the Bridgewater Canal. On the way you pass the River Irwell and the now little used Pomona and Manchester Docks.

WALKING INSTRUCTIONS - From Castlefields Junction, follow the signs for the Roman Fort and Science Museum and walk along Duke Street to Liverpool Road. Turn left passing the Science and Industry Museum on your right. At the end turn left along Water Street and left again along Dawson street. After passing under the railway bridge take the second road on your right - Ellesmere Street - and pass the star Inn on your left. Turn right along Hulme Hall Road and cross the canal to the Ribble Bus Company. Bear left passing under a railway and soon following a track with the canal on your left. Turn left over the first bridge - Cornbrook Bridge - and walk along the towpath with the canal on your right. To the right is the Pomona Docks and the Colgate and Palmolive works. After 1/2 mile gain the main road (A5063). Turn right over the bridge and at the end turn left to gain the towpath. The canal is now on your left and keep on the towpath for the next 1 1/2 miles to Water's Meeting Junction. On your left is Old Trafford and on your right Kraft Foods. At the junction bear right along the Bridgewater Canal to the first bridge - Taylor's Bridge; cross it and turn left to continue along the towpath.

CASTLEFIELDS - Britain's first urban Heritage Park. A massive development area being restored and more than a day can be spent exploring the Waterways area, Roman Fort, River Irwell and Salford Quays and the galleries and museums including the Museum of Science & Industry - Europe's largest museum. The Grocers Warehouse at the end of the Bridgewater Canal is part of the development.

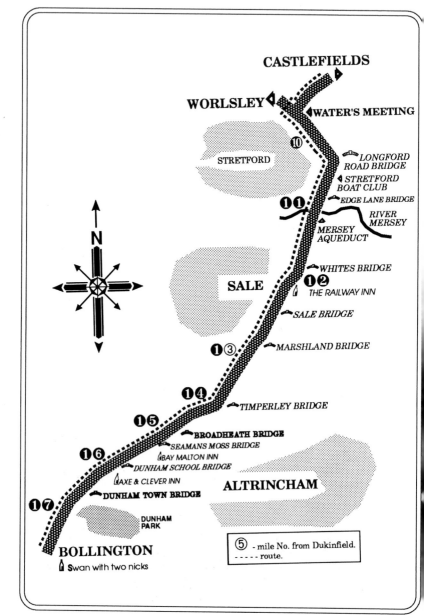

THE BRIDGEWATER CANAL
WATER'S MEETING
TO BOLLINGTON - 7 1/2 miles

CASTLEFIELDS

WORLSLEY

WATER'S MEETING

STRETFORD

LONGFORD ROAD BRIDGE

STRETFORD BOAT CLUB

EDGE LANE BRIDGE

RIVER MERSEY

MERSEY AQUEDUCT

WHITES BRIDGE

SALE

THE RAILWAY INN

SALE BRIDGE

MARSHLAND BRIDGE

TIMPERLEY BRIDGE

BROADHEATH BRIDGE

SEAMANS MOSS BRIDGE

BAY MALTON INN

DUNHAM SCHOOL BRIDGE

AXE & CLEVER INN

ALTRINCHAM

DUNHAM TOWN BRIDGE

DUNHAM PARK

BOLLINGTON

Swan with two nicks

⑤ - mile No. from Dukinfield.
- - - - - route.

22

WATER'S MEETING TO BOLLINGTON - 7 1/2 MILES

allow 2 1/4 hours.

CANAL - Bridgewater.

 - O.S. 1:50,000 Landranger Series Sheet No 109 - Manchester & surrounding area.

ABOUT THE SECTION - First you walk through the suburbia of Stretford and its boating club. After two miles you leave the buildings behind and cross the Mersey Aqueduct before passing under the M63 motorway. Afterwards you re-enter suburbia as you pass through Sale and Timperley; but it is an attractive section with railway stations every mile. The final three miles of this stage are in delightful countryside with canalside pubs and small villages along the way. Near Bollington is Dunham Park and Bollington village is just down the lane from the canal; the inn is called "Swan with two Nicks". You will walk above another Bollington when you walk along the Macclesfield Canal north of Macclesfield.

WALKING INSTRUCTIONS - From Water's Meeting continue on the towpath, on the righthand side of the canal. Keep on this path for the entire section to Bollington

❋❋❋❋❋❋❋❋

DUNHAM PARK - Deer park now National Trust property. The 18th century hall, Dunham Massey, was the former home of the Earl of Stamford.

Bridgewater Canal - Sale.

THE BRIDGEWATER CANAL
BOLLINGTON TO PRESTON BROOK - 12 1/2 miles

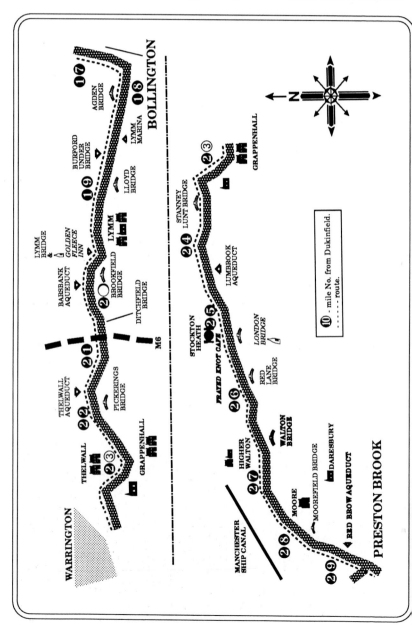

BOLLINGTON

⑰

AGDEN BRIDGE

⑱

LYMM MARINA

BURFORD UNDER BRIDGE

⑲

LLOYD BRIDGE

LYMM BRIDGE & GOLDEN FLEECE INN

BARSBANK AQUEDUCT

BROOKFIELD BRIDGE

②⓪

LYMM

DITCHFIELD BRIDGE

M6

THELWALL AQUEDUCT

②①

PICKERINGS BRIDGE

②②

THELWALL

②③

GRAPPENHALL

WARRINGTON

GRAPPENHALL

②③

STANNEY LUNT BRIDGE

②④

LUMBROOK AQUEDUCT

STOCKTON HEATH

②⑤

FRIED KNOT CAFE

LONDON BRIDGE

②⑥

RED LANE BRIDGE

WALTON BRIDGE

HIGHER WALTON

②⑦

MOORE

②⑧

MANCHESTER SHIP CANAL

MOOREFIELD BRIDGE

DARESBURY

◄ RED BROW AQUEDUCT

②⑨

PRESTON BROOK

⑩ - mile No. from Dukinfield.
- - - - - route.

BOLLINGTON TO PRESTON BROOK - 12 1/2 MILES

- allow 3 1/2 hours.

CANAL - BRIDGEWATER

   - O.S. 1:50,000 Landranger Series Sheet No 109 - Manchester
& surrounding area.
   - O.S. 1:50,000 Landranger Series Sheet No 108 - Liverpool
& surrounding area.

ABOUT THE SECTION - Mostly rural walking with the canal, as usual, carving a peaceful haven through the modern world. First you pass through Lymm before reaching Stockton Heath and the southern edge of Warrington. All the time the Manchester Ship Canal is within a mile. Beyond Warrington (Higher Walton) you begin heading southwards as you reach the south-western corner of the route. In four miles you are at Preston Brook and the Trent & Mersey Canal. On the right is the five mile Runcorn branch of the Bridgewater Canal. This is a very pleasant stage of the circuit and a curtain raiser to what is to come. Now that the confines of Manchester are behind you the rest of the circuit to Dukinfield is a truly magnificent walk through canal scenery second to none.

WALKING INSTRUCTIONS - From Bollington continue along the towpath on the righthand side of the canal. Follow this the whole way to Preston Brook.

✳✳✳✳✳✳✳

Agden Bridge - Bridgewater Canal.

25

Bridgewater Canal - Lymm.

Bridgewater Canal - Grappenhall.

Bridgewater Canal - London Bridge Inn, Stockton Heath.

Preston Brook.

TRENT & MERSEY CANAL

First known as the Grand Trunk. - was authorised on 14th May 1766 with a capital of £150,000. James Brindley surveyed the route 93 3/8 miles from Derwent Mouth on the Trent to Preston Brook on the Bridgewater Canal near Runcorn. Work began immediately and by 1777 the whole canal was open with 76 locks.

The principal movers in the project were Erasmus Darwin and Josiah Wedgwood who saw it as a need for the Potteries and Midlands area. The major problem in construction was the 2,900 yard long Harecastle Tunnel. Many were skeptical that the canal company would ever pay a dividend but in 1781 5% was paid and in 1825 a £100 share was worth £2,300. The canal was used considerably for the transport of clay and flint for the pottery works around Stoke on Trent. It was not until late last century that transportation rapidly declined.

The Shardlow area is covered fully in Volume One of this series. The Stoke on Trent section is particularly interesting having the remarkable Harecastle Tunnel and is described in Volume Two of this series. Volume Seven will deal with the whole of the canal from end to end - a magnificent week's walk!

The original Harecastle Tunnel was built by James Brindley, took eleven years to construct, and is now closed. The tunnel - 9 feet wide and 1 3/4 miles long - was an unprecedented undertaking in the late 18th Century. There was no towpath and horses had to be led over the hill while the boat was legged through. As a result there was a considerable time loss while boats were moved through. In 1822 Thomas Telford suggested that another tunnel be constructed next to the existing one, and this was completed in 1827 with towpath. The two tunnels then operated on a one-way system , greatly reducing the traffic congestion. Mining subsidence gradually made Brindley's tunnel unusable and by 1918 it had been abandoned. By the 1950s the other tunnel was suffering from subsidence and part of the towpath had to be removed. Between 1973-1977 the tunnel was closed for major repairs but is once again operational. Plaques on the southern entrance record the tunnel's history and a canal milepost that once stood on the horse path is now here.

The canal is often referred to as the Grand Canal, because nine other canals radiate from it, including the Coventry Canal and the Staffordshire & Worcestershire Canal.

Claymore Navigations, Preston Brook.

Trent & Mersey Canal milepost.

Preston Brook Tunnel.

29

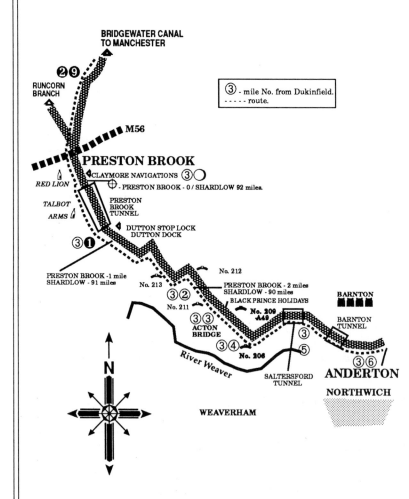

BRIDGEWATER CANAL
TO MANCHESTER

②⑨

RUNCORN
BRANCH

M56

③ - mile No. from Dukinfield.
- - - - - route.

PRESTON BROOK

RED LION

CLAYMORE NAVIGATIONS ③◯

⊕ - PRESTON BROOK - 0 / SHARDLOW 92 miles.

TALBOT
ARMS

PRESTON
BROOK
TUNNEL

DUTTON STOP LOCK
DUTTON DOCK

③❶

PRESTON BROOK -1 mile
SHARDLOW - 91 miles

No. 213

No. 212

③②

No. 211

PRESTON BROOK - 2 miles
SHARDLOW - 90 miles

BLACK PRINCE HOLIDAYS

BARNTON

③③

ACTON
BRIDGE

No. 209
A49

BARNTON
TUNNEL

③④

No. 206

③

River Weaver

⑤

SALTERSFORD
TUNNEL

③⑥

ANDERTON

N

NORTHWICH

WEAVERHAM

CANAL - Trent & Mersey.

O.S. 1:50,000 Landranger Series sheets Nos. -

108 - Liverpool & surrounding area.
117 - Chester, Wrexham & surrounding area.
118 - Stoke on Trent & Macclesfield area.

ABOUT THE SECTION - A quite outstanding section of canal throughvery attractive scenery with three tunnels - Preston Brook, Saltersford and Barnton - to walk over. The section ends at one of the most impressive canal features anywhere in the world, the Anderton Lift to the River Weaver. Plans are afoot to bring this masterpiece back to working order. The Trent & Mersey Canal is one of Britain's finest canals and this section amply demonstrates its unique character and why it is so appreciated by all. You will also note that the canal has mileposts showing the mileage from Preston Brook and Shardlow. To the thru hiker this can be a little upsetting seeing how far is still to go! The bridges are also numbered, unlike the Bridgewater Canal where they are named.

WALKING INSTRUCTIONS - For the whole section you follow the towpath on the righthand side of the canal. Soon after leaving Preston Brook you will have to ascend over Preston Brook tunnel, crossing the A533 road beside the Talbot Arms before regaining the canal 1/2 mile later. Four miles later walk over Saltersford Tunnel and Barton Tunnel 1/4 mile later. Less than a mile later reach the Anderton Lift.

THE ANDERTON BOAT LIFT - Was opened in 1875 and is in all probability the finest piece of canal engineering in Britain today. Prior to its construction there was considerable trade on the Trent & Mersey Canal and the River Weaver, fifty feet below; especially salt. Goods were manhandled between the two and shoots were built to slide the salt down, but it was still very labour intensive. The lift was originally hydraulically operated. A canal boat entered the top of the lift in its own water, into a watertight tank. Another boat on the River Weaver would enter a similar tank and by releasing a small amount of water to make the upper tank heavier, the boats would descend and rise, passing each other. The tanks are 75 feet long by 15 feet 6 ins wide and fully loaded with water weighed 252 tons. In 1908 the lift was converted to electrical power and 250 ton counterweights were added; and the whole structure was strengthened. Plans are underway to totally restore the lift to working order and build a Visitor's Centre.

PRESTON BROOK - Built especially for the Trent & Mersey Canal. Here goods were transferred to narrowboats.

NORTHWICH - The town's coat or arms says, "Sal est Vita", meaning Salt is Life. Salt has been mined here since Roman times.

Trent & Mersey Canal at Anderton Lift.

Anderton Lift.

Barnton Tunnel - Trent & Mersey Canal.

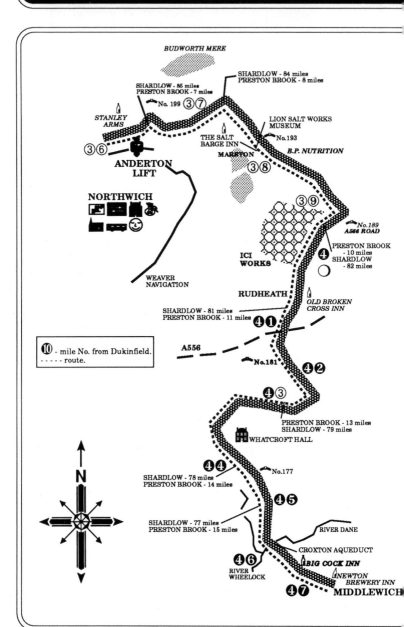

BUDWORTH MERE

SHARDLOW - 84 miles
PRESTON BROOK - 8 miles

SHARDLOW - 85 miles
PRESTON BROOK - 7 miles
No.199 ③⑦

STANLEY
ARMS

③⑥

**ANDERTON
LIFT**

NORTHWICH

THE SALT
BARGE INN
MARSTON

LION SALT WORKS
MUSEUM
No.193

B.P. NUTRITION

③⑧

③⑨

No.189
A556 ROAD

PRESTON BROOK
- 10 miles
SHARDLOW
- 82 miles

④

**ICI
WORKS**

WEAVER
NAVIGATION

RUDHEATH

OLD BROKEN
CROSS INN

SHARDLOW - 81 miles
PRESTON BROOK - 11 miles
④①

⑩ - mile No. from Dukinfield.
- - - - - route.

A556

No.181 ④②

④③

PRESTON BROOK - 13 miles
SHARDLOW - 79 miles

WHATCROFT HALL

④④

SHARDLOW - 78 miles
PRESTON BROOK - 14 miles

No.177

④⑤

SHARDLOW - 77 miles
PRESTON BROOK - 15 miles

RIVER DANE

CROXTON AQUEDUCT

④⑥
RIVER
WHEELOCK

BIG COCK INN

*NEWTON
BREWERY INN*

④⑦ **MIDDLEWICH**

N

ANDERTON TO MIDDLEWICH - 9 MILES
- allow 3 hours.

CANAL - *Trent & Mersey.*

 - 0.5. 1:50,000 Landranger Series Sheet No 118 - Stoke on Trent & Macclesfield area.

ABOUT THE SECTION - The canal nearly encircles Northwich and for the first 4 miles there is much industry, especially in the latter half, between Marston and Rudheath. At Marston is the Lion Works, an old salt works. The section from Rudheath to Middlewich is very Pleasant countryside with the River Dane close by. You cross this before Middlewich on the Croxton Aqueduct. Many miles later near the Bosley Locks, Congleton, you cross the River Dane again on an aqueduct. The river has its source high up on the moorlands of the Peak District near the Cat & Fiddle Inn. There are several inns in the Northwich area and more again at Middlewich.

WALKING INSTRUCTIONS - No problems on this section; the towpath is well defined and keeps on the righthand side of the canal. Follow it all the way to Middlewich, to the locks, Bridge No 169 and the Middlewich Branch of the Shropshire Union Canal.

MIDDLEWICH - Salt has mined here since Roman times and evidence of their occupation still remain. The Roman forces were paid in salt - called "Sal dare", from which the name soldier is derived. The "wich" in the name is derived from "Wych" the Celtic n~me connected with salt. Middlewich is the middle wich of Nantwich in the south and Northwich in the north.

Lion Salt Works, Marston - Trent & Mersey Canal.

I.C.I. Works, Northwich - Trent & Mersey Canal.

King's Lock Inn, Middlewich - Trent & Mersey Canal

Locks near Harding's Wood - Trent & Mersey Canal.

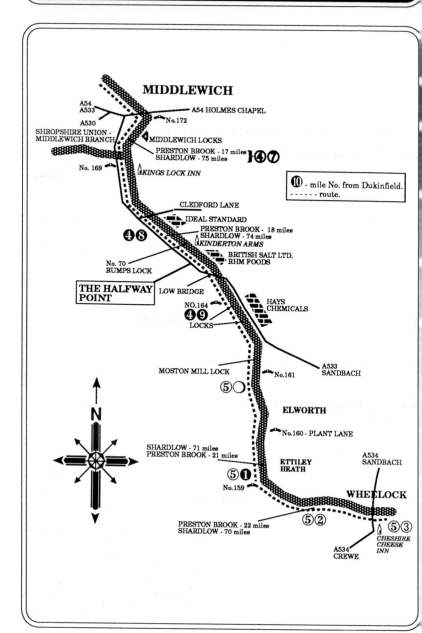

THE TRENT & MERSEY CANAL
MIDDLEWICH TO HARDINGS WOOD
JUNCTION - 14 miles - (Map 1)

MIDDLEWICH

A54
A533
A530

SHROPSHIRE UNION -
MIDDLEWICH BRANCH

No. 169

A54 HOLMES CHAPEL

No.172

MIDDLEWICH LOCKS

PRESTON BROOK - 17 miles
SHARDLOW - 75 miles

❿④⑦

KINGS LOCK INN

❿ - mile No. from Dukinfield.
- - - - - route.

CLEDFORD LANE

IDEAL STANDARD

④⑧

PRESTON BROOK - 18 miles
SHARDLOW - 74 miles
KINDERTON ARMS

BRITISH SALT LTD.
RHM FOODS

No. 70
RUMPS LOCK

THE HALFWAY POINT

LOW BRIDGE

HAYS
CHEMICALS

NO.164

④⑨

LOCKS

MOSTON MILL LOCK

No.161

A533
SANDBACH

⑤○

ELWORTH

No.160 - PLANT LANE

SHARDLOW - 71 miles
PRESTON BROOK - 21 miles

ETTILEY
HEATH

A534
SANDBACH

⑤❶

No.159

WHEELOCK

PRESTON BROOK - 22 miles
SHARDLOW - 70 miles

⑤②

⑤③

CHESHIRE
CHEESE
INN

A534
CREWE

38

MIDDLEWICH TO HARDINGS WOOD JUNCTION - 14 MILES
allow 5 hours.

CANAL - Trent & Mersey.

O.S. 1:50,000 Landranger Series Sheet No 118 - Stoke on Trent & Macclesfield area.

ABOUT THE SECTION - The longest section of the route but an extremely fine one. First you pass the Middlewich locks and walk close to the A533 road for 2 1/2 miles before entering delightful countryside and passing the canal side inns at Wheelock. Here the locks change to double ones, easing the passage for the narrowboats. The locks also lead out of the Cheshire Plain. As you head nearer to Hardings Wood the edge of the Pennines becomes more pronounced and the Mow Cop folly is a noticeable landmark. At Hardings Wood - your most southern point - you leave the Trent & Mersey Canal and head north to Dukinfield!

WALKING INSTRUCTIONS - Continue along the towpath on the righthand side of the canal for the next ten miles. En route passing through Wheelock, Hassall Green, and Rode Heath. 1/2 mile later at Lock No 49 cross the canal and continue with the canal on your right on the defined towpath. Continue through Red Bull and underneath the aqueduct to Hardings Wood Junction - the -junction of the Macclesfield and Trent & Mersey Canals. You will cross the aqueduct soon as you begin following the Macclesfield Canal. If time permits it is worth continuing a little further to see the famed Harecastle tunnel

SANDBACH - In the cobbled Market Square are two Saxon crosses of the 8th century.

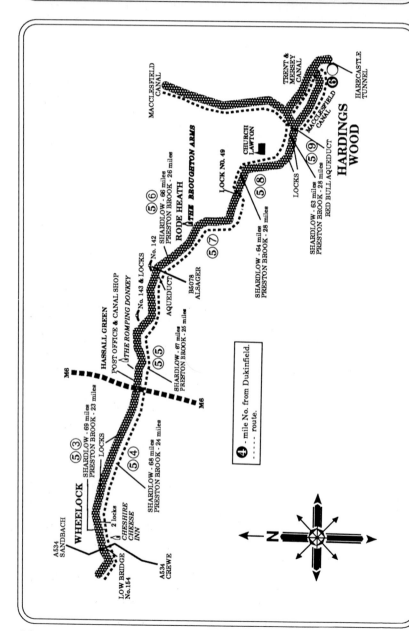

THE TRENT & MERSEY CANAL
MACCLESFIELD CANAL
HARECASTLE TUNNEL
HARDINGS WOOD
MACCLESFIELD CANAL
CHURCH LAWTON
LOCK NO. 49
THE BROUGHTON ARMS
RODE HEATH
No. 142
No. 143 & LOCKS
AQUEDUCT
B5078 ALSAGER
SHARDLOW - 66 miles
PRESTON BROOK - 26 miles
SHARDLOW - 67 miles
PRESTON BROOK - 25 miles
SHARDLOW - 63 miles
PRESTON BROOK - 28 miles
RED BULL AQUEDUCT
SHARDLOW - 64 miles
PRESTON BROOK - 28 miles
LOCKS
HASSALL GREEN
POST OFFICE & CANAL SHOP
THE ROMPING DONKEY
M6
M6
SHARDLOW - 69 miles
PRESTON BROOK - 23 miles
LOCKS
WHEELOCK
SHARDLOW - 68 miles
PRESTON BROOK - 24 miles
A534 SANDBACH
2 locks
CHESHIRE CHEESE INN
LOW BRIDGE No.154
A534 CREWE

mile No. from Dukinfield.
----- route.

40

Hardings Wood Junction - Macclesfield Canal and the Trent & Mersey Canal.

Harecastle Tunnel - Trent & Mersey Canal.

MACCLESFIELD CANAL

Authorised by Act in 1826 it was fully operational in 1831 and is 27 3/4 miles long with 13 locks. The basic line was surveyed by Thomas Telford but the canal engineer was William Crosley. The canal joins the Peak Forest Canal near Marple in the north and leaves the Trent & Mersey at Hardings Wood Junction near Kidsgrove.

The canal is one of the most attractive passing beneath the final hills of the Pennines, where the Cheshire Plain begins. Basically on a south to north axis the canal passes Congleton and through Macclesfield and Bollington following a largely straight course, with impressive embankments and aqueducts, especially at Bollington and Hardings Wood. The canal does a sharp turn at Bosley where twelve locks are located with the rocky hill of The Cloud standing guard.

Although one of the last canals to be constructed, the canal saw extensive use in the 19th century despite competition from the railways - the canal was bought by the Great Central Railway Company, who also purchased the Peak Forest and Ashton canals. By the end of the century like all canals traffic had steadily declined. This century saw its continued decline and as the Peak Forest and Ashton canals were out of use, the Macclesfield Canal was no longer a through route. In the 1960's it was little used but a decade later with the restoration of the Peak Forest and Ashton canals the canal has been transformed into one of the most interesting. The Macclesfield Canal also has the honour of being the first canal to have a canal boat club - the North Cheshire Cruising Club - founded in 1943.

Macclesfield Canal milepost.

Crossover bridge - Macclesfield Canal.

Hovis Mill and Macclesfield Marina - Macclesfield Canal

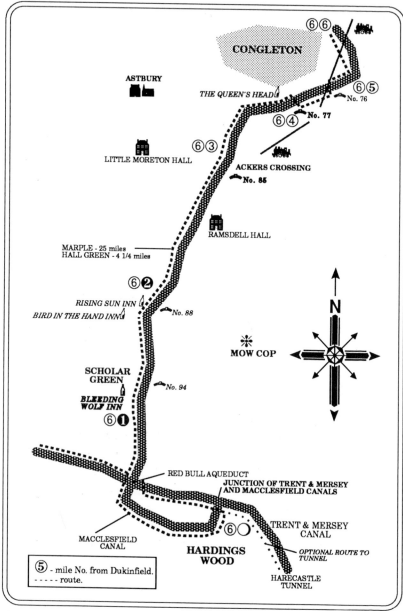

THE MACCLESFIELD CANAL
HARDINGS WOOD JUNCTION
TO CONGLETON - 6 miles

CONGLETON

ASTBURY

THE QUEEN'S HEAD

⑥⑥

⑥⑤ No. 76

⑥④ No. 77

⑥③

LITTLE MORETON HALL

ACKERS CROSSING
No. 85

RAMSDELL HALL

MARPLE - 25 miles
HALL GREEN - 4 1/4 miles

⑥❷

RISING SUN INN
BIRD IN THE HAND INN
No. 88

N

MOW COP

SCHOLAR
GREEN
No. 94

BLEEDING
WOLF INN

⑥❶

RED BULL AQUEDUCT

JUNCTION OF TRENT & MERSEY
AND MACCLESFIELD CANALS

MACCLESFIELD
CANAL

⑥○

TRENT & MERSEY
CANAL

HARDINGS
WOOD

OPTIONAL ROUTE TO
TUNNEL

HARECASTLE
TUNNEL

⑤ - mile No. from Dukinfield.
- - - - - route.

44

CANAL - Macclesfield.

 - O.S. 1: 50,000 Landranger series sheet No 118 - Stoke on Trent & Macclesfield area.

ABOUT THE SECTION - After crossing the Red Bull Aqueduct the canal is dominated by Mow Cop to the east. The canal is full of interest, passing first through Scholar Green and on past Ramsdell Hall on the righthand side. A little further is the path to the left to Little Moreton Hall. The edge of the Pennines remain on your right and nearing Congleton the rugged slopes of The Cloud become pronounced.

WALKING INSTRUCTIONS - At Hardings Wood Junction cross over to the start of the Macclesfield Canal and follow the towpath looping back on yourself before crossing the Trent & Mersey via Red Bull Aqueduct. The towpath keeps to the lefthand side of the canal and you follow it for the next 5 miles to bridge No 77 on the outskirts of Congleton. Cross over to the other side and continue to the next bridge No 76; a classic example of a crossover bridge. Cross over and continue with the canal on your righthand side

❖❖❖❖❖❖

CONGLETON - A former textile town with several half-timbered buildings and a Venetian Gothic Town Hall. The town's origins date back to Neolithic times. From the 17th century onwards it has been known as the Bear Town. Before the annual wakes one year the bear died. Rather than disappoint everyone money put aside to purchase a new bible was used to buy another bear. Hence the rhyme - *"Congleton rare Congleton rare, sold the bible to buy a bear"*.

RODE HALL - 18th century country house near Scholar Green.

MOW COP - 1,000 feet above sea level and a magnificent viewpoint over the Cheshire Plain stands the folly known as Mow Cop Castle, built in 1750 by Randle Wilbraham. The summit had a Beacon Tower and was used to signal the Spanish Armada, but has long since gone. Close by is the rock pinnacle known as the Old Man of Mow Cop and both now belong to the National Trust. A stone beneath the "castle" records the site was used in 1807 for the first meeting of the Primitive Methodists. The Staffordshire Way (92 miles) and the Mow Cop Trail starts from here.

LITTLE MORETON HALL - Dating from the 16th century it is a stunning moated manor house and one of the best examples of black and white design in the country. The property is now cared for by the National Trust and contains an exceptional cobbled courtyard, well tended gardens and numerous rooms rich in carvings, including the long gallery, 68 feet long by 12 feet wide.

Typical Trent & Mersey Canal milepost.
- at Hardings Wood.

Trent & Mersey Canal from Red Bull Aqueduct.

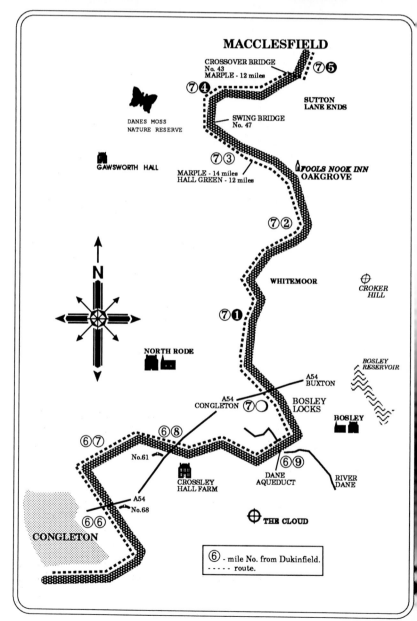

THE MACCLESFIELD CANAL
CONGLETON
TO MACCLESFIELD - 10 MILES

MACCLESFIELD

CROSSOVER BRIDGE
No. 43
MARPLE - 12 miles

⑦❺

⑦❹

SUTTON
LANE ENDS

DANES MOSS
NATURE RESERVE

SWING BRIDGE
No. 47

GAWSWORTH HALL

⑦③

MARPLE - 14 miles
HALL GREEN - 12 miles

FOOLS NOOK INN
OAKGROVE

⑦②

WHITEMOOR

CROKER
HILL

N

⑦❶

NORTH RODE

BOSLEY
RESERVOIR

A54
BUXTON

A54
CONGLETON ⑦◯

BOSLEY
LOCKS

BOSLEY

⑥⑦

⑥⑧

No.61

BphOSLEY

⑥⑨

DANE
AQUEDUCT

RIVER
DANE

CROSSLEY
HALL FARM

A54
No.68

⑥⑥

CONGLETON

THE CLOUD

⑥ - mile No. from Dukinfield.
- - - - - route.

48

CANAL - Macclesfield.

 O.S. 1:50,000 Landranger Series Sheet No. 118 - Stoke on Trent & Macclesfield area.

ABOUT THE SECTION - An outstanding section of canal walking. First skirting Congleton before walking beneath the slopes of The Cloud to the River Dane Aqueduct. The next mile is breathtaking as you ascend past the Bosley Locks. Beyond the peaceful canal passes Oakgrove and three miles later at Gurnett you cross over and continue on the other side of the canal to central Macclesfield. The section ends at the impressive Hovis Mill and Macclesfield Marina.

WALKING INSTRUCTIONS - Continue on the lefthand side of the canal as you head northwards. First beneath The Cloud, then over the Dane Aqueduct, past the Bosley Locks, and beyond Oakgrove after nearly 8 miles from Congleton, reach Bridqe No 43 and cross over to the righthand side. Continue along the towpath and more than a mile later reach the Macclesfield Marina and former Hovis Mill on your left, just before the A537 road where there is the Puss and Boots Inn and Bridgewater Arms.

✳✳✳✳✳✳✳

MACCLESFIELD (Centre) - ten minutes walk from Bridge No 37 is the Heritage Centre and Paradise Mill. Silk weaving was the principal industry here from 1750 onwards. The last handloom buisness ceased in 1981. Paradise Mlll, a Victorian silk Mill, has been reopened as a working museum and is open most days.

GAWSWORTH HALL - The hall and church date from Norman times but the current buildings date from the 15th century. The hall was built by the Fitton family who were renowned for their jousting. The grounds include one of the finest tilting arenas in England - 200 yards long by 60 yards wide. Members of the family include Mary Fytton, known as the "Dark Lady" of Shakespeare's Sonnets. The hall is open to the public and the church is located above one of the five ponds and is particularly attractive.

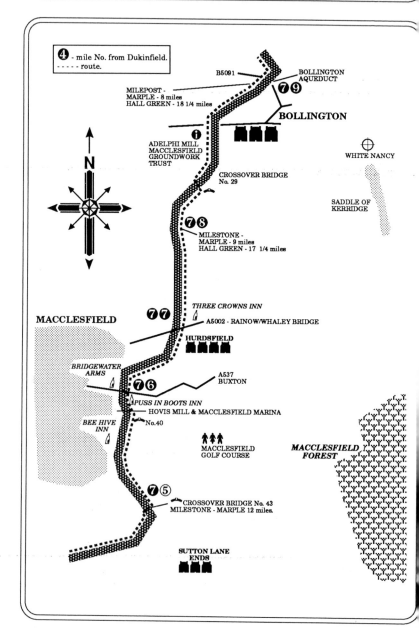

THE MACCLESFIELD CANAL
MACCLESFIELD TO MARPLE
JUNCTION - 11 miles (MAP 1)

4 - mile No. from Dukinfield.
- - - - - route.

B5091

BOLLINGTON AQUEDUCT

7 9

MILEPOST -
MARPLE - 8 miles
HALL GREEN - 18 1/4 miles

BOLLINGTON

N

i

WHITE NANCY

ADELPHI MILL
MACCLESFIELD
GROUNDWORK
TRUST

CROSSOVER BRIDGE
No. 29

SADDLE OF
KERRIDGE

7 8

MILESTONE -
MARPLE - 9 miles
HALL GREEN - 17 1/4 miles

MACCLESFIELD

7 7

THREE CROWNS INN

A5002 - RAINOW/WHALEY BRIDGE

HURDSFIELD

*BRIDGEWATER
ARMS*

7 6

A537
BUXTON

PUSS IN BOOTS INN
HOVIS MILL & MACCLESFIELD MARINA

*BEE HIVE
INN*

No.40

MACCLESFIELD
GOLF COURSE

*MACCLESFIELD
FOREST*

7 5

CROSSOVER BRIDGE No. 43
MILESTONE - MARPLE 12 miles.

SUTTON LANE
ENDS

50

MACCLESFIELD TO MARPLE JUNCTION - 11 MILES
- allow 4 hours.

CANAL - Macclesfield.

 - O.S. 1:50,000 Landranger Series Sheet Nos. -

118 - Stoke on Trent & Macclesfield area.

109 - Manchester & surrounding area.

ABOUT THE SECTION - Another superlative section! First past the slopes of Kerridge Hill and on above Bollington and over impressive aqueducts and past the Adelphi Mill. The remainder is through peaceful quiet countryside, with the Middlewood Way close by, to Marple Junction - the junction with the Peak Forest Canal, the last canal of the circuit!

WALKING INSTRUCTIONS - From Macclesfield Marina continue on the towpath (righthand side) with the canal on your left, for the next 1 1/2 miles. After passing the canal milepost - Marple 9 miles/ Hall Green 17 1/4 miles - reach Bridge No 29, a crossover bridge. Cross to the other side of the canal and keep the canal on your right for the next 9 miles, passing Bollington, and High Lane. On reaching the fringe of Marple cross bridge No 2 to the right passing the Ring o' Bells Inn and turn left to cross another bridge and so gain Marple Junction and the Peak Forest Canal.

BOLLINGTON - dominated by the 1,000 foot high ridge of Kerridge, the town had numerous mills, driven by the many streams and later by coal carried on the canal. The last cotton mill ceased operating in 1960. The Kerridge Hill has the renowned landmark - White Nancy. This is believed to have been built by the Gaskell family to commemorate the Battle of Waterloo, and Nancy was a member of the family. The houses are built from stone quarried from the Kerridge Hill.

THE MIDDLEWOOD WAY - 11 miles from Marple to Macclesfield. A former railway line - the M,B and M railway (Macclesfield, Bollington and Marple.) Built in the 1860's it was never a great success and in 1970 it was closed to both passenger and goods trains. The Macclesfield Borough and Stockport Metropolitan Borough Councils worked together to change the line to a leisureway for walkers, cyclists and riders, and it was opened in 1985.

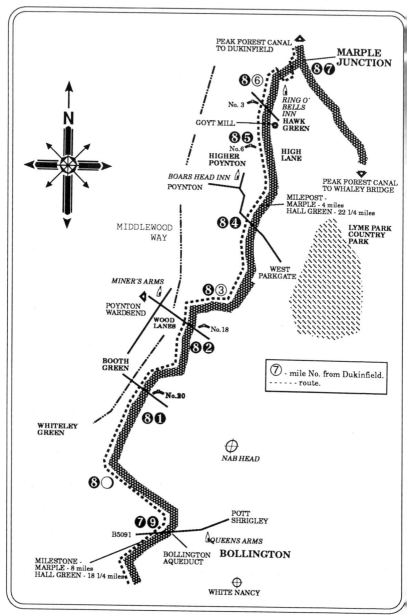

PEAK FOREST CANAL TO DUKINFIELD

MARPLE JUNCTION

⑧⑦

⑧⑥

No. 3

RING O' BELLS INN

GOYT MILL

HAWK GREEN

⑧⑤

HIGH LANE

No.6

HIGHER POYNTON

BOARS HEAD INN

POYNTON

⑧④

PEAK FOREST CANAL TO WHALEY BRIDGE

MILEPOST - MARPLE - 4 miles
HALL GREEN - 22 1/4 miles

MIDDLEWOOD WAY

LYME PARK COUNTRY PARK

MINER'S ARMS

⑧③

WEST PARKGATE

POYNTON WARDSEND

WOOD LANES

No.18

⑧②

BOOTH GREEN

No.20

| ⑦ - mile No. from Dukinfield. |
| - - - - - route. |

⑧①

WHITELEY GREEN

⊕ NAB HEAD

⑧○

⑦⑨

POTT SHRIGLEY

B5091

↟QUEENS ARMS

BOLLINGTON

BOLLINGTON AQUEDUCT

MILESTONE - MARPLE - 8 miles
HALL GREEN - 18 1/4 miles

⊕ WHITE NANCY

Macclesfield Canal near Sutton Lane Ends.

Bollington Aqueduct from the road - Macclesfield Canal.

PEAK FOREST CANAL

Authorised by Act of Parliament in 1794 the canal was completed, with the exception of the Marple locks in 1800. 14 1/2 miles long from Whaley Bridge to its junction with the Ashton canal at Dukinfield. The 16 Marple Locks took four years to construct during which time a temporary tramway linked the canal together. The canal engineer was Benjamin Outram, one of the founders of Butterley Ironworks in Derbyshire.

The prime use of the canal was for the transportation of limestone from the Buxton/Doveholes area. The Bugsworth (Buxworth) basin was constructed with tramway from the quarry. Here at Bugsworth stone was either tipped into a boat or lime kiln. The scene was a busy one with boats bringing coal for the kilns. The whole Bugsworth site is Particularly interesting and is currently being restored. The Whaley Bridge terminus was linked to the Cromford Canal - engineered by William Jessop and Benjamin Outram In 1794 - by the Cromford and High Peak Railway engineered by Josiah Jessop, the son of William, and completed in 1825. There were several schemes for joining the two canals together but because of the hilly terrain of the Peak District, a railway with nine inclines seemed the best practical solution.

The Peak Forest Canal runs through idyllic scenery from the Peak District hills to the fringe of Manchester. The canal is full of features including the 16 locks at Marple and the famous Marple Aqueduct over the river Goyt, 100 feet below. Beyond is the 308 feet long Hyde Bank Tunnel, which has to be walked over as no towpath exists. The Woodley tunnel a little further north is 176 yards long and complete with towpath.

By the middle of the 19th century the canal was losing its trade to the railways and traffic dwindled. Even so Buxworth was still being used until 1922 and the section northwards from Marple Junction was in use until the mid 1930's. The section of the canal from Whaley Bridge towards Marple was still usable in the 1960's but the rest became derelict. Ten years later it had been restored and is now part of the Cheshire Ring.

On May 13th 1974 the Cheshire Ring was complete by the reopening of the lower Peak Forest Canal from the Marple locks to the Portland Basin at Dukinfield, and the Ashton Canal from here to Ducie Street Junction (Rochdale Canal). A distance of 14 1/4 miles with 34 locks.

Marple Locks - Peak Forest Canal.

Marple Aqueduct over River Goyt - Peak Forest Canal.

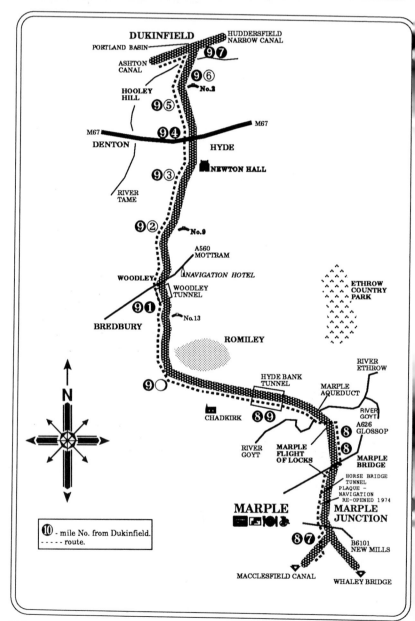

THE PEAK FOREST CANAL
MARPLE JUNCTION
TO DUKINFIELD - 10 miles

DUKINFIELD

HUDDERSFIELD NARROW CANAL

PORTLAND BASIN

⑨⑦

ASHTON CANAL

⑨⑥

No.2

HOOLEY HILL

⑨⑤

M67

⑨④

M67

DENTON

HYDE

■NEWTON HALL

⑨③

RIVER TAME

⑨②

No.9

A560 MOTTRAM

NAVIGATION HOTEL

WOODLEY

Woodley Tunnel

⑨①

BREDBURY

No.13

ROMILEY

ETHROW COUNTRY PARK

HYDE BANK TUNNEL

RIVER ETHROW

MARPLE AQUEDUCT

⑨〇

RIVER GOYT

CHADKIRK

⑧⑨

A626 GLOSSOP

⑧

RIVER GOYT

MARPLE FLIGHT OF LOCKS

⑧

MARPLE BRIDGE

HORSE BRIDGE TUNNEL PLAQUE – NAVIGATION RE-OPENED 1974

MARPLE

MARPLE JUNCTION

⑩ - mile No. from Dukinfield.
- - - - - route.

⑧⑦

B6101 NEW MILLS

MACCLESFIELD CANAL

WHALEY BRIDGE

56

MARPLE JUNCTION TO DUKIN-FIELD - 10 MILES

allow 3 1/2 hours

CANAL - Peak Forest.

  O.S. 1:50,000 Landranger Series Sheet No 109 - Manchester & surrounding area.

ABOUT THE SECTION - The last one of the circuit and the finest! You start at Marple Junction and the top of the flight of Marple Locks. After passing through a remarkable horse tunnel you descend the locks to the Marple Aqueduct; a stunning architectural feature. Next you walk through Hyde Bank Tunnel and 2 miles later the Woodley Tunnel. You are now entering the Greater Manchester area but the canal still retains its rural character as you walk the final steps to Dukinfield, where you began a few days or weeks ago. It is a fitting end to a very satisfying walk.

WALKING INSTRUCTIONS - From Marple Junction continue northwards beside the Peak Forest Canal on your right, passing through the famed horse tunnel. Pass locks 16 to 9 and at the A626 road, (Bridge 17) cross over and gain the towpath on the righthand side of the canal. Begin descending past further locks of the Marple flight and after the last one cross Bridge 16 and follow the towpath on your left. You now cross the Marple Aqueduct and go through the Hyde Bank Tunnel. Two miles later pass through the Woodley Tunnel. The next 1 1/2 miles the River Tame is on your left. At Bridge No 7 cross over to the righthand side and little over 1/2 mile later at Bridge No 6, Hyde, cross over for the last time and walk along the towpath on the lefthand side of the canal. Portland Basin is less than 3 miles away and you simply follow the towpath back to Dukinfield where you began.

Marple Locks - Peak Forest Canal.

Woodley Tunnel - Peak Forest Canal.

Portland Basin, Dukinfield - Junction of - Peak Forest Canal, Ashton Canal and Huddersfield Narrow Canal.

Horse Bridge - Dukinfield - Peak Forest Canal.

AMENITIES GUIDE -

TOWN/ VILLAGE	B & B	INN	CAMP SITE	REST- AURANT	SHOP	P.O.	YHA
DUKINFIELD	■	■			■		
DROYISDEN		■			■		
OPENSHAW		■					
BESWICK		■					
MANCHESTER	■	■		■	■	■	
SALE	■	■		■	■	■	
OLDFIELD BROW		■					
DUNHAM TOWN	■	■					
BOLLINGTON		■					
LYMM	■	■			■		
GRAPPENHALL		■					
STOCKTON HEATH		■			■	■	
HIGHER WALTON		■					
DARESBURY		■					
RUNCORN	■	■		■	■	■	
PRESTON BROOK		■			■		
DUTTON		■					
BARNTON		■					
ANDERTON		■					
NORTHWICH	■	■		■	■	■	
MARSTON		■					
BROKEN CROSS		■					
MIDDLEWICH	■	■		■	■	■	
WHEELOCK	■	■	■		■	■	
HASSALL GREEN		■	■				
RODE HEATH		■					
HARDINGS WOOD		■		■	■	■	
HALL GREEN		■					
KENT GREEN		■					
CONGLETON	■	■	■	■	■	■	
OAKGROVE		■					
MACCLESFIELD	■	■		■	■	■	
BOLLINGTON	■	■			■	■	

AMENITIES GUIDE -

TOWN/ VILLAGE	B & B	INN	CAMP SITE	REST- AURANT	SHOP	P.O.	YHA
HIGHER POYNTON		■			■		
HIGH LANE		■			■	■	
MARPLE	■	■		■	■	■	
ROMILEY		■					
WOODLEY		■			■		
HYDE		■			■	■	

Old Broken Cross Inn, Rudheath,

AMENITIES GUIDE

INNS

DROYLSDEN - Cotton Tree
Church Hotel

OPENSHAW - Yew Tree
The Friendship
Crabtree
Inns Church
Bridge Inn

BESWICK - Navigation
Alexandra

CENTRAL MANCHESTER - New Union Inn

SALE - Bridge Inn (Dane Road Bridge)
The Railway (Sale Bridge)

OLDFIELD BROW - Bay Malton (Seamons Moss Bridge)

DURHAM TOWN - Axe & Cleaver

BOLLINGTON -- Swan with Two Nicks
Ye Olde No 3

LYMM - Golden Fleece
Bull's Head
Spread Eagle

GRAPPENHALL - Ram's Head
Parr Arms

STOCKTON HEATH - London Bridge

HIGHER WALTON - Walton Arms

DARESBURY - Ring o' Bells

RUNCORN - The Barge Hotel
Egerton Arms
Clarendon

PRESTON BROOK - Red Lion

DUTTON - Talbot Arms

BARNTON - Red Lion

ANDERTON - Stanley Arms

MARSTON - New Inn

BROKEN CROSS - Old Broken Cross

MIDDLEWICH - Kinderton Arms
King's Lock
Big Lock
Newton Brewery Inn
Cheshire Cheese

WHEELOCK (Near Sandbach) - Cheshire Cheese

HASSALL GREEN - The Romping Donkey

RODE HEATH - Broughton Arms
Royal Oak

HARDINGS WOOD - The Tavern
Blue Bell
Red Bull
Canal Tavern

HALL GREEN - Bleedlng Wolf Inn

KENT GREEN - Bird in Hand
Rising Sun
Three Horseshoes

CONGLETON - The Wharf
The Railway
The Queen's Head

OAKGROVE - Fool's Nook

MACCLESFIELD - Puss in Boots Inn (Bridge 37)
Bridgewater Arms (Bridge 37)
Georqe & Draqon (Bridqe 34)

BOLLINGTON - Dog and Partridge
The Vale
Windmill (Bridge 25)
Miner's Arms (Bridge 18)

HIGHER POYNTON - Boars Head (Bridge 15)
HIGH LANE - Bull's Head
Dog & Partridge
MARPLE - Ring o' Bells
Navigation
ROMILEY - Waterside Restaurant
The Railway
WOODLEY - Navigation
HYDE - Cheshire Ring Hotel (Bridge No 6)
DUKINFIELD - The Globe (Bridge No 2 Peak Forest Canal)

AMENITIES GUIDE

BED AND BREAKFAST

The following is a random selection. Many of the inns beside the canal provide accommodation. Central Manchester has numerous hotels.

DUKINFIELD - *Cheshire Ring Hotel (East of bridge)*

ALTRINCHAM - *Mrs. M. Jennings, Castle Hill Farm, Ringway, Altrincham. Tel. 061-928-1155. Snacks available if required.*

Mrs. Jackson, Tanyard Farm, Ashley, Altrincham. Tel. 061-928-1009. Tea and coffee making facilities. Separate lounge with Colour TV for guests.

TATTON PARK - *Mrs. Reeves, Tatton Dale Farm, Tatton Park, Knutsford. Tel. Knutsford 0565 - 54692*

PICKMERE - *Mrs. Brown, Pickmere House, Park Lane, Pickmere. Tel. 056589 - 3433*

MIDDLEWICH - *Mrs. Susan Moss, Forge Mill Farm, Warmingham. Tel. 027077 - 204. Evening Meals 6-7 p.m..*

- Mrs. F.M. Williams, Curtis Hulme Farm, Bradwell Rd., Middlewich, CW10 0LD. Tel. 060684 - 3230

SANDBACH - *Mrs. J. Coulson, 104 Congleton Road, Sandbach. CW11 0DQ Tel. 0270 - 760056*

WHEELOCK - *Mrs. S. Furber, 44 Hind Heath Road, Wheelock, Sandbach. CW11 9LY Tel. 0270 - 762702*

CONGLETON - *Mrs. V. Edwards, Greenacres, 48 Camborne Close, Congleton. Tel. 0260-271899. Approx. 3/4 mile from town centre in quiet cul-de-sac overlooking canal.*

Mrs. M.C. Downs, Cuttleford Farm, Newcastle Road, Astbury, Congleton. Tel. 0260-272499. Opposite Little Moreton Hall on A34 four miles south of Congleton.

BOSLEY - *Mrs. M Whittaker, Lower House Farm, Bosley. Tel. North Rode 02603 - 318*

MACCLESFIELD - Mrs. D.B. smith, 'Belle Grove', 237 Park Lane, Macclesfield. Tel. 0625-613003. (Opposite entrance to South Park.) 1 family room that sleeps 4/S, also cottage annexes .

Chester House, Chestergate. Tel. 0625-23709.

MARPLE-BRIDGE - Mrs. M. Sidebottom/ Shire Cottager Benches Lane, Marple-Bridge. Tel. 061-427 2377 or 045745-66536. (Opposite Woodheys Farm Restaurant) Evening meal available 6.30 p.m.

CAMPING

There are few camping sites close to the canal and the Ring is not really suitable for backpacking. A shame really. When I hiked the Rideau Trail in southern Ontario, Canada ,you were able to camp beside the Rideau Canal at the locks; perhaps a thought for the future?

HASSALL GREEN - Mr. P. Colclough, Roughwood Farm, Nr. Sandbach. Tel. Alsager 872079. open all year.

SANDBACH - Mr. and Mrs. Parton, Woodyfields Farm, Malkins Bank.
Tel. Crewe 762185. Open all year.

CONGLETON - Mr. and Mrs. Olliver, Shannock Farm, Somerford Booths, Congleton. Tel. Congleton 276357. Open all year.

Golden Fleece Inn, Lymm - Bridgewater Canal.

CANAL FEATURES - to look for

STOP PLANKS - *in various places can be seen vertical grooves in the canal walls - especially near bridges - with handled planks stacked nearby. The planks are slotted into the grooves sealing the canal while repairs or cleaning of the drained section is carried out.*

ROPE GROOVES - *on the side of bridges, sometimes with either cast iron or wooden shields, can be seen the grooves cut by the horse tow lines over the decades, such as the photograph below at Ditchfield Bridge, Bridgewater Canal.*

TURNOVER/CROSSOVER BRIDGES - *in a few places the tow-path switches sides of the canal and a bridge was built to enable the horse to cross over without unhitching the line. The Macclesfield Canal has several splendid examples.*

SWING BRIDGES - *as the name implies, the bridge could be swung out of the way to allow boats to pass.*

BALANCED BRIDGES - *bridges finely balanced that can be either pushed upwards out of the way or lowered across the canal.*

SKEW BRIDGES - *most canal bridges are built at right angles to the canal. In a few cases to avoid the Z bend in the road the bridge was built at an angle.*

Rope grooves at Ditchfield bridge Bridgewater Canal

CANAL MUSEUMS

1. The Canal and National Waterways Museum,
The Boat Museum,
Dockyard Road,
Ellesmere Port,
South Wirral.
L65 4EF
Tel. No 051-355 5017

2. British Waterways Board,
   Waterways Museum,
   Stoke Bruerne,
   Towcester,
   Northants.

3. The National Waterways Museum,
   Llanthony Warehouse,
   Gloucester Docks,
   Gloucester.
   GL1 2EH

   Tel. No. 0452-25524

OTHERS OF RELATED INTEREST -

1. Paradise Mill,
   Park Lane,
   Macclesfield.
   Cheshire. SK11 6TJ
tel. No 0625-618228

2. Silk Museum,
   The Macclesfield Heritage Centre,
   Roe Street,
   Macclesfield.
   Cheshire. SK11 6UT
tel. No. 0625-613210

3. Brindley Mill and Museum,
   Mill Street,
   Leek.
   Staffordshire

4. Groundwork Discovery Centres at
a. Adelphi Mill, Bollington. (Macclesfield Canal).
 b. Lion Salt Works, Marston, Northwich. (Trent & Mersey Canal)

5. Greater Manchester Museum of Science & Industry,
Castlefields.

✿✿✿✿✿✿✿✿✿✿✿✿✿

CANAL SOCIETIES & USEFUL ADDRESSES -

British Waterways Board,
Information Centre,
Melbury House,
Melbury Terrace,
London .
NW1 6JX

Ashton Canal,
Tudor Cruising Club,
C. Brooks,
5 Livingstone Street,
Leeds, Oldham,
Greater Manchester. OL4 5BY

Northwich Area Engineer,
Navigation Road,
Northwich, Cheshire.

Huddersfield Canal Society,
R.A. Dewey,
38, Paris Road,
Scholes,
Huddersfield.
West Yorkshire.

Macclesfield Canal Society,
 D. Rushton,
72, Blakelow Road,
Macclesfield.
Cheshire.
SK11 7ED

Peak Forest Canal Society,
T. Reeve,
12 Rushton Drive,
Marple,
 Cheshire. SK6 7LX

Trent & Mersey Canal Society,
M. Mitchell,
34, Kennedy Avenue,
Long Eaton,
Nottingham.

SUGGESTED FURTHER READING
- a Random selection.

"The Canals of the East Midlands" Charles Hadfield David & Charles
"The Canals of the West Midlands" Charles Hadfield David & Charles
"British Canals - an Illustrated History" Charles Hadfield David & Charles 1979
"James Brindley" H. Bode Shlre Publictions 1973
"The Trent & Mersey Canal" Lindsay David & Charles 1979
Nicholson/Ordnance Survey Guide to the Waterways - Vol 2 Central
Nicholson/Ordnance Survey Gulde to the Waterways - Vol 3 - North
Cheshire Ring Canal Walk - Vols 1 to11 - Cheshire County Council publications.
Canal Companlon Cheshire Rlng J.M.Pearson 1986
"Discovering Canals in Britain" Peter L.Smith Shire Publications
"Discovering Lost Canals" Ronald Russell Shire Publications
"Inland Cruising" Tom Willis Pelham Books

OTHER CANAL WALK BOOKS
BY JOHN N. MERRILL

Vol 1 - Derbyshire and Nottinghamshire.
- more than 30 walks on the Chesterfield, Cromford, Erewash, Nutbrook, Derby, Nottingham and Trent & Mersey Canals.

Vol 2 - Cheshire and Staffordshire.
- More than 40 walks on the Peak Forest, Macclesfield, Caldon and Trent & Mersey canals.

VOL 3 - Staffordshire.
- More than 30 walks on the Trent & Mersey, Staffordshire & Worcestershlre, and Coventry canals.

Vol 6 - South Yorkshire.
- 25 walks on the Barnsley, Dove & Dearne, River Don and Navigation, New Junction , and Staniforth and Keadby Canals.

FORTHCOMING -

Vol 5 - Nottinghamshire, Leicestershire and Lincolnshire.
- deals with River Trent, Grantham Canal, River Soar, Witham Navigation, and Foss Dyke Navigation.

Vol 7 - The Trent & Mersey Canal
- end to end walk.

Vol 8 & 9 - Birmingham Canals - North & South

Goldren Shred Works, Droylsden, Ashton Canal.

LOG

DATE STARTED...

DATE COMPLETED..

ROUTE POINT	MILE NO.	ARR.	DEP.	COMMENTS WEATHER
DUKINFIELD	0			
AUDENSHAW	1			
FAIRFILED LOCK	2			
CLAYTON LOCKS	3			
BESWICK LOCKS	5 1/2			
DUCIE STREET JNC	6			
CASTLEFIELDS	7			
CORNBROOK BR.	8			
KRAFT FOODS	9			
WATER'S MEETING	10			
MERSEY AQUEDUCT	11			
WHITES BRIDGE	12			
MARSHLAND BR.	13			
TIMPERLEY BRIDGE	14			
BROADHEATH BR.	15			

LOG

DATE STARTED...

DATE COMPLETED...

ROUTE POINT	MILE NO.	ARR.	DEP.	COMMENTS WEATHER
DUNHAM SCH BR.	16			
BOLLINGTON	17 1/2			
AGDEN BRIDGE	18			
LLOYD BRIDGE	19			
BARSBANK AQUE.	20			
M6 BRIDGE	21			
GRAPPENHALL	23			
STOCKTON HEATH	25			
HIGHER WALTON	27			
PRESTON BROOK	29 1/2			
CLAYMORE NAVI.	30			
DUTTON LOCK	31			
ACTON BRIDGE	33			
SALTERSFORD TUN.	35			
ANDERTON LIFT	36 1/2			

LOG

DATE STARTED..

DATE COMPLETED..

ROUTE POINT	MILE NO.	ARR.	DEP.	COMMENTS WEATHER
MARSTON	38			
ICI WORKS	40			
A556	41			
CROXTON AQUE.	46			
MIDDLEWICH	47			
IDEAL STANDARD	48			
HAYS CHEMICALS	49			
ETTILEY HEATH	51			
WHEELOCK	53			
M6 BRIDGE	54 1/2			
RODE HEATH	57			
CHURCH LAWTON	58			
RED BULL AQUE.	59			
HARDINGS WOOD JUNCTION	60			
SCHOLAR GREEN	61 1/2			

LOG

DATE STARTED...

DATE COMPLETED...

ROUTE POINT	MILE NO.	ARR.	DEP.	COMMENTS WEATHER
RAMSDELL HALL	62 1/2			
QUEEN'S HEAD	64			
CONGLETON	66			
A54 (BR.61)	68			
DANE AQUEDUCT	69			
BOSLEY LOCKS	70			
OAKGROVE	72 1/2			
SUTTON LANE ENDS	75			
MACCLESFIELD	76			
BOLLINGTON AQUE.	79			
WOODS LANE	82			
GOYT MILL	85			
MARPLE JUNCTION	87			
HYDE BANK TUNNEL	89			
DUKINFIELD	97			

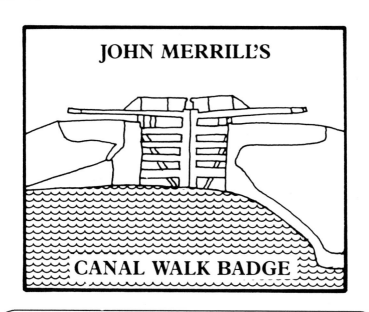

JOHN MERRILL'S

CANAL WALK BADGE

JOHN MERRILL'S CANAL WALK BADGE

Badges are blue cloth with lock gates embroidered in four colours and measure - 3 1/2" wide x 2" high.

BADGE ORDER FORM

Dates of walk..

NAME...

ADDRESS..

..

Price: £2.00 each including postage, VAT and signed completion certificate.

From: J.N.M. Publications, Winster, Matlock, Derbyshire, DE4 2DQ Tel: Winster (062988) 454 - 24hr answering service. Fax: Winster (062988) 416

********* *You may photocopy this form if needed* ********

THI JOHN MERRILL WALK BADGE - walk this route twice or complete another John Merrill's challenge walk and send details and cheque/PO for £2.00 for a special circular walk badge. Price includes postage and VAT.

EQUIPMENT NOTES

Some personal thoughts

BOOTS - *preferably with a full leather upper, of medium weight, with a vibram sole. I always add a foam cushioned insole to help cushion the base of my feet.*

SOCKS - *I generally wear two thick pairs as this helps minimise blisters. The inner pair are of loop stitch variety and approximately 80% wool. The outer are a thick rib pair of approximately 80% wool.*

WATERPROOFS - *for general walking I wear a T shirt or cotton shirt with a cotton wind jacket on top. You generate heat as you walk and I prefer to layer my clothes to avoid getting too hot. Depending on the season will dictate how many layers you wear. In soft rain I just use my wind jacket for I know it quickly dries out. In heavy or consistant rain I slip on a neoprene lined gagoule, and although hot and clammy it does keep me reasonably dry. Only in extreme conditions will I don overtrousers, much preferring to get wet and feel comfortable. I never wear gaiters!*

FOOD - *as I walk I carry bars of chocolate, for they provide instant energy and are light to carry. In winter a flask of hot coffee is welcome. I never carry water and find no hardship from not doing so, but this is a personal matter! From experience I find the more I drink the more I want and sweat. You should always carry some extra food such as Kendal Mint Cake, for emergencies.*

RUCKSACKS - *for day walking I use a climbing rucksack of about 40 litre capacity and although it leaves excess space it does mean that the sac is well padded, with an internal frame and padded shoulder straps. Inside apart from the basics for one day I carry gloves, balaclava, spare pullover and a pair of socks.*

MAP & COMPASS - *when I am walking I always have the relevant map - preferably 1:25,000 scale - open in my hand. This enables me to constantly check that I am walking the right way. In case of bad weather I carry a compass, which once mastered gives you complete confidence in thick cloud or mist.*

REMEMBER AND OBSERVE THE COUNTRY CODE

 Enjoy the countryside and respect its life and work.

 Guard against all risk of fire.

Fasten all gates.

 Keep your dogs under close control.

 Keep to public paths across farmland.

Use gates and stiles to cross fences, hedges and walls.

  Leave livestock, crops and machinery alone.

 Take your litter home - pack it in; pack it out.

 Help to keep all water clean.

 Protect wildlife, plants and trees.

 Take special care on country roads.

THE HIKER'S CODE

✿ Hike only along marked routes - do not leave the trail.

✿ Use stiles to climb fences; close gates.

✿ Camp only in designated campsites.

✿ Carry a light-weight stove.

✿ Leave the trail cleaner than you found it.

✿ Leave flowers and plants for others to enjoy.

✿ Keep dogs on a leash.

✿ Protect and do not disturb wildlife.

✿ Use the trail at your own risk.

✿ Leave only your thanks and footprints - take nothing but photographs.

OTHER BOOKS by JOHN N. MERRILL PUBLISHED by JNM PUBLICATIONS

CIRCULAR WALK GUIDES -
SHORT CIRCULAR WALKS IN THE PEAK DISTRICT
LONG CIRCULAR WALKS IN THE PEAK DISTRICT
CIRCULAR WALKS IN WESTERN PEAKLAND
SHORT CIRCULAR WALKS IN THE STAFFORDSHIRE MOORLANDS
SHORT CIRCULAR WALKS AROUND THE TOWNS & VILLAGES OF
THE PEAK DISTRICT
SHORT CIRCULAR WALKS AROUND MATLOCK
SHORT CIRCULAR WALKS IN THE DUKERIES
SHORT CIRCULAR WALKS IN SOUTH YORKSHIRE
SHORT CIRCULAR WALKS AROUND DERBY
SHORT CIRCULAR WALKS AROUND BUXTON
SHORT CIRCULAR WALKS IN THE HOPE VALLEY
40 SHORT CIRCULAR WALKS IN THE PEAK DISTRICT
CIRCULAR WALKS ON KINDER & BLEAKLOW
SHORT CIRCULAR WALKS IN SOUTH NOTTINGHAMSHIRE
SHIRT CIRCULAR WALKS IN CHESHIRE

CANAL WALKS -
VOL 1 - DERBYSHIRE & NOTTINGHAMSHIRE
VOL 2 - CHESHIRE & STAFFORDSHIRE
VOL 3 - STAFFORDSHIRE
VOL 4 - THE CHESHIRE RING
VOL 5 - LINCOLNSHIRE & NOTTINGHAMSHIRE
VOL 6 - SOUTH YORKSHIRE
VOL 7 - THE TRENT & MERSEY CANAL

JOHN MERRILL DAY CHALLENGE WALKS -
WHITE PEAK CHALLENGE WALK
DARK PEAK CHALLENGE WALK
PEAK DISTRICT END TO END WALKS
STAFFORDSHIRE MOORLANDS CHALLENGE WALK
THE LITTLE JOHN CHALLENGE WALK
YORKSHIRE DALES CHALLENGE WALK
NORTH YORKSHIRE MOORS CHALLENGE WALK
LAKELAND CHALLENGE WALK

INSTRUCTION & RECORD -
HIKE TO BE FIT.....STROLLING WITH JOHN
THE JOHN MERRILL WALK RECORD BOOK

MULTIPLE DAY WALKS -
THE RIVERS'S WAY
PEAK DISTRICT: HIGH LEVEL ROUTE
PEAK DISTRICT MARATHONS
THE LIMEY WAY
THE PEAKLAND WAY

COAST WALKS & NATIONAL TRAILS -
ISLE OF WIGHT COAST PATH
PEMBROKESHIRE COAST PATH
THE CLEVELAND WAY

PEAK DISTRICT HISTORICAL GUIDES -
DERBYSHIRE INNS - an A to Z guide
HALLS AND CASTLES OF THE PEAK DISTRICT & DERBYSHIRE
TOURING THE PEAK DISTRICT & DERBYSHIRE BY CAR
DERBYSHIRE FOLKLORE
PUNISHMENT IN DERBYSHIRE
CUSTOMS OF THE PEAK DISTRICT & DERBYSHIRE
WINSTER - a souvenir guide
ARKWRIGHT OF CROMFORD
TALES FROM THE MINES by Geoffrey Carr
PEAK DISTRICT PLACE NAMES by Martin Spray

JOHN MERRILL'S MAJOR WALKS -
TURN RIGHT AT LAND'S END
WITH MUSTARD ON MY BACK
TURN RIGHT AT DEATH VALLEY
EMERALD COAST WALK

COLOUR GUIDES -
THE PEAK DISTRICT.........Something to remember her by.

SKETCH BOOKS -
NORTH STAFFORDSHIRE SKETCHBOOK by John Creber

IN PREPARATION -
LONG CIRCULAR WALKS IN STAFFORDSHIRE
SHORT CIRCULAR WALKS IN WEST YORKSHIRE
SHORT CIRCULAR WALKS IN THE YORKSHIRE DALES
SHORT CIRCULAR WALKS IN THE LAKE DISTRICT
SHORT CIRCULAR WALKS IN NORTH YORKSHIRE MOORS
RUTLAND WATER CHALLENGE WALK
SNOWDONIA CHALLENGE WALK
FOOTPATHS OF THE WORLD - Vol 1 - NORTH AMERICA
HIKING IN NEW MEXICO

☞ *Full list from JNM PUBLICATIONS, Winster, Matlock, Derbys.*